GRAB A SEAT AT THE
PERIODIC TABLE!

A CHEMICAL MYSTERY

© 2008 Weldon Owen Education Inc. All rights reserved.

No part of this publication may be reproduced or transmitted
in any form or by any means, electronic or mechanical,
including photocopying, recording, taping, or any information storage
and retrieval system, without permission in writing from the publisher.

Library of Congress Cataloging-in-Publication Data

Strom, Laura Layton.
  Grab a seat at the periodic table! : a chemical mystery / By Laura
  Layton Strom.
      p. cm. -- (Shockwave)
  Includes index.
  ISBN-10: 0-531-17793-9 (lib. bdg.)
  ISBN-13: 978-0-531-17793-8 (lib. bdg.)
  ISBN-10: 0-531-15481-5 (pbk.)
  ISBN-13: 978-0-531-15481-6 (pbk.)

  1. Periodic law--Juvenile literature. 2. Chemical elements--Juvenile
literature. 3. Detective and mystery stories--Juvenile literature.
I. Title. II. Series.

  QD467.S77 2008
  546'.8--dc22

2007014769

Published in 2008 by Children's Press, an imprint of Scholastic Inc.,
557 Broadway, New York, New York 10012
www.scholastic.com

SCHOLASTIC, CHILDREN'S PRESS, and associated logos are trademarks
and/or registered trademarks of Scholastic Inc.

08 09 10 11 12 13 14 15 16 17
10 9 8 7 6 5 4 3 2 1

Printed in China through Colorcraft Ltd., Hong Kong

Author: Laura Layton Strom
Educational Consultant: Ian Morrison
Editor: Mary Atkinson
Designer: Pirzad Rustomjee
Photo Researcher: Jamshed Mistry
Illustrations by: Scott Pearson/Visual Evolution

Photographs by: Big Stock Photo (skull X-ray, p. 19; pp. 22– 23; coin, p. 24; metals, p. 25;
gold bars, pp. 26–27; water, p. 28); **Getty Images** (cover; pp. 10–11); **Jennifer and Brian Lupton**
(teenagers, pp. 32–33); **Photodisc** (p. 5; nebula, pp. 14–15); **Photolibrary** (pp. 8–9; pp. 16–17;
manufacturing silicon chips, pp. 18–19; amethyst crystals, p. 21; alchemists, pp. 24–25; salt
crystal, pp. 28–29; p. 30; particle accelerator, pp. 32–33); **Tranz/Corbis** (p. 3; p. 7; Superman,
p. 15; chemist, pp. 20–21; bronze head, p. 25; p. 27; woman, p. 29)

All illustrations and other photographs © Weldon Owen Education Inc.

GRAB A SEAT AT THE PERIODIC TABLE!

A CHEMICAL MYSTERY

Laura Layton Strom

children's press®

An imprint of Scholastic Inc.

NEW YORK • TORONTO • LONDON • AUCKLAND • SYDNEY
MEXICO CITY • NEW DELHI • HONG KONG
DANBURY, CONNECTICUT

CHECK THESE OUT!

SHOCKER
Stuff to Shock, Surprise, and Amaze You

Quick Recaps and Notable Notes

Word Stunners and Other Oddities

The Heads-Up on Expert Reading

Links to More Information

CONTENTS

atom the smallest amount of an element that still has the properties of that element

element a substance, such as oxygen or gold, that cannot be split into a simpler substance

lab short for laboratory; a place in which scientists conduct experiments and study their results

molecule (*MOL uh kyool*) the smallest part of a substance into which it can be divided while still being that same substance

periodic table of elements a chart that lists all the known elements in an ordered way. The elements are placed in relation to one another according to their shared properties.

properties the characteristics or traits of a substance

· ·

For additional vocabulary, see Glossary on page 34.

Some words tell a bit about people's beliefs. The word *atom* comes from the Greek *atemmein*, meaning "not cut." It was once thought that the atom could not "be cut" because nothing could be smaller.

Look around you. Most of the things that you can see are made up of smaller parts. A rock, for example, is not just a rock. It might be made up of several different substances, such as quartz and silica. Or think of a cake. It's not just a cake. It is a combination of ingredients, such as flour, sugar, eggs, and milk. We can break down these ingredients even further. For example, one cake ingredient, sugar, is made up of three **elements**: hydrogen, carbon, and oxygen.

Some scientists specialize in food chemistry. They investigate ways of improving the foods that we buy in stores.

Chemists are scientists who study substances. They often break down a substance into its most basic parts. This way, they can determine which elements make up the substance. Chemists also study the **properties** of substances. Their discoveries allow us to use and understand substances better.

Helium is an invisible gas. It is lighter than air, which is why helium-filled balloons rise upward.

Aluminum is a **metal**. It is strong, light, and **malleable**.

Sulfur crystals are bright yellow. Sulfur gas smells like rotten eggs.

Carbon has different forms. The soft, dark graphite in pencils is one form. Diamond and charcoal are other forms.

Oxygen is an invisible gas in the air. Humans breathe in oxygen. It then combines with carbon inside our bodies to become a gas called carbon dioxide.

IT BEGAN WITH A BANG

"Weird!" exclaimed Celia, as she entered the science **lab**.

"Not normal!" said Kenny, following her into the room.

Today was the first day of school, and the students were already getting some strange feelings about their new science class. As they filed in, they noticed that the tables weren't arranged in even rows. Instead, they were grouped in an unusual shape. Each place was labeled with one or two bold letters and tiny numbers. Celia pointed to a notice on the whiteboard. She saw *Ca* next to her name, so she took her place at the seat by that label. Kenny followed her lead and sat at seat *K*.

"What does *K* mean?" asked Kenny. "Hey, maybe I'm *K*ing of the class!"

"I thought that the labels were made up of the first one or two letters in our names," said Celia. "But the second letter in my name is *e* not *a*!" The other students murmured to each other and took their places. Then came the explosion!

Part of these pages seems to be fiction, while the other part contains facts. I wonder whether this pattern continues. It certainly makes the book more interesting.

Welcome!

1. Here's how out to figure out where you sit. Find your name on the list. Note the letter or letters beside it.
2. Look at the classroom plan below. Find the table labeled with your letter or letters. That is where you sit!

Al	Allie	B	Bart	Be	Ben	C	Cai	Ca	Celia
Cl	Cleo	Co	Colin	Cr	Cora	Cu	Curt	F	Fiona
Fe	Ferran	Ga	Gaia	Ge	Geraldo	H	Hanna	He	Hector
K	Kenny	Li	Lisa	Mg	Maggie	Mn	Mandisa	N	Nadia
Na	Nathan	Ne	Neville	Ni	Nina	O	Owen	P	Paige
S	Sandeep	Sc	Scott	Si	Sienna	V	Victor		
Ti	Tim	Zn	Zane						

H																	He
Li	Be											B	C	N	O	F	Ne
Na	Mg											Al	Si	P	S	Cl	
K	Ca	Sc	Ti	V	Cr	Mn	Fe	Co	Ni	Cu	Zn	Ga	Ge				

THE MYSTERY

The storeroom door opened, and out walked a woman in a white lab coat. She held a ripped plastic sandwich bag in her gloved hands. Her hair was short, spiked, and black. She wore green safety glasses over her red eyeglasses. She grinned widely, obviously proud of the noise that she'd made.

"Good morning, class! I hope you are awake now. I find a mixture of baking soda, vinegar, and warm water gets my mornings started with a bang. Well, I'm Ms. **Solution**. I know what you're thinking – *Solution* is a lucky name for a science teacher!" Suddenly the class was aware of an odor wafting out of the bag. Ms. Solution took a whiff.

"Yummy, smells like baking! Anyway, now that you're awake, let's try to solve an important mystery! It baffled scientists for centuries!" She pointed to a question she'd written earlier on a whiteboard.

"What is all **matter** in the universe made of?" she read out. "Start thinking about this question. We will be investigating it further."

SHOCKER

An explosion is a kind of **chemical reaction**. When baking soda and vinegar mix, they give off a lot of gas. If the reaction happens in a sealed bag, the bag will explode when there is more gas than the bag can hold.

What is all matter in the universe made of?

air?

water?

chemicals?

cloth?

atoms?

ELEMENTary Fact

When baking soda and vinegar mix, bubbles of carbon dioxide form almost instantly. Ask an adult to help you see this for yourself. Be sure to wear safety glasses! First, put a spoonful of vinegar into a deep bowl. Then add a spoonful of baking soda, and watch the action!

IT'S ELEMENTARY!

"You've noticed that your desks are in a fascinating arrangement," said Ms. Solution. The students nodded. "Actually, for our classroom arrangement to be perfect, we would need more than 100 seats. However, we have only 31 students, so we will work with that.

The word *elementary* means "first" or "beginning." This helps us figure out what the word *element* means. An element is a substance that cannot be broken down into a simpler substance.

"Each of your desk labels stands for something important. For example, will Hanna and Hector please come to the front of the class? Bring your labels with you."

Hanna and Hector jumped to their feet.

"When we look at the whole universe, about 97 percent of it is made up of Hanna and Hector," Ms. Solution said. The class giggled.

"Hanna's H symbol stands for hydrogen. Hector's He stands for helium. The rest of you are probably wondering what your labels mean. Some of you are very common. Some of you are very rare. You all occur in nature, though some others are made by humans.

"Puzzled? It's elementary, really. All of you are elements on the **periodic table of elements**!

"Now, for homework, I'd like each of you to find out the name of your element. Please write the name on your label."

This image was taken by the Hubble Space Telescope. It shows a huge pillar of hydrogen (H) gas and dust in space. Each of the finger-like projections at the top is about the size of our solar system!

2
He

SHOCKER

The element calcium (C) is a metal. It is found in teeth and bones. We drink it in milk. However, it is also used to help make cement, fertilizer, and insecticide!

ELEMENTary Fact

Krypton (Kr) is a real element, not just something from Superman stories. Krypton is a gas used in some lightbulbs and laser beams. Krypton lasers are used in eye surgery. Krypton is also found on Mars!

PROBING DEEPER

On Tuesday, Ms. Solution thanked the students for finding out the names of their elements.

"Was anyone surprised by what he or she found?" she asked.

Kenny raised his hand. "Yes, Kenny?"

"I thought mine would be an element that starts with the letter K – something like Kennyite." The class snickered.

"Ah," said Ms. Solution, "I'm not surprised you were confused. Some of the elements are hard to figure out. Your element is named for a Latin word, *kalium*, which we call potassium. Tricky!

"Scientists name the elements they discover. They also study how elements look, smell, feel, and act. They want to know how the elements act alone, and how they react with others. These 'personality traits' are called properties. Other properties of elements include their **mass** and **density**.

"Today, we are all detectives." Ms. Solution continued. "You're on a mission. You need to scour books and Web sites to uncover the properties of your element. What does it look like, smell like, and act like? How does it react when it combines with other elements? Write your findings in your notebooks."

19 K
Potassium

16

A HAZMAT (hazardous materials) response team investigates a chlorine-gas leak.

Some Properties of Chlorine (Cl)

- Chlorine is a foul-smelling, greenish-yellow gas.

- In nature, chlorine is always found combined with other elements.

- Chlorine gas is heavier than air. Escaped chlorine gas sinks to form a layer below the air.

- Inhaling chlorine gas harms the breathing passages of animals and people.

- Chlorine in water can kill germs, such as **bacteria**. This is why small amounts of chlorine are often put into drinking water and swimming pools.

Properties of Elements
- Look
- Smell
- Feel
- Mass
- Density
- Action and reaction

Some Properties of Potassium (K)

- Potassium is a lightweight, silver-colored **metallic** element.

- It is soft enough to cut with a knife.

- In nature, potassium is always found combined with other elements.

- Pure potassium bursts into flame when exposed to dry air, and it **dissolves** in water.

- Potassium is an important mineral for human health. Foods such as bananas and potatoes contain potassium.

Potassium burning in air

17

THE CROSSWORD PUZZLE

The next day, everyone quickly took their seats at the periodic table of elements. Ms. Solution emerged from the storeroom with two rolls of paper towels.

"I hope we aren't cleaning the lab," whispered Gaia.

Ms. Solution made her way over to Ben and handed him a roll with blue flowers. "Ben, I'd like you to unravel your roll. Pass it along until you reach Celia."

The students unrolled the paper as instructed. When they were done, Ms. Solution continued. "OK, everyone holding the blue-flowered paper towel is in the same group on the periodic table. Think of it as a crossword puzzle. The groups are the 'down' columns. Everyone in a group has something in common. So Ben's beryllium (Be), Maggie's magnesium (Mg), and Celia's calcium (Ca) have something in common. Let's look in your chemistry books, and find out what these elements have in common."

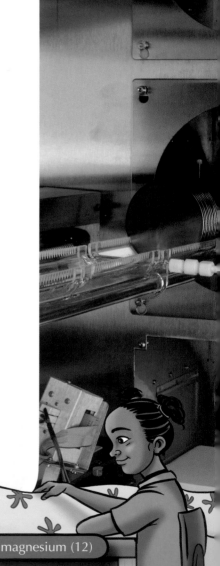

beryllium (4)

magnesium (12)

Manufacturing silicon chips

Elements are classified as metals, **nonmetals**, or **semimetals**. Most natural elements are metals. They are shiny and **conduct** electricity. Nonmetals are brittle or waxy, or they are gases. Most cannot conduct electricity. The semimetals have properties of metals and nonmetals. Silicon, for example, is a semimetal. It is not shiny like a metal. However, it can conduct a weak electric charge. Silicon is used to make computer chips.

What do the elements beryllium (Be), magnesium (Mg), and calcium (Ca) have in common?

Answer:
They are part of a group called the **alkaline** earth metals.

In nature, they are usually found combined with other substances.

They are soft, shiny metals.

They all react with water to give off hydrogen gas.

ELEMENTary Fact

Your body has metal in it – and that's not counting your braces! The most common metal in the body is calcium. An adult body can contain more than 2 pounds of calcium. Most of it is in the bones and teeth.

calcium (20)

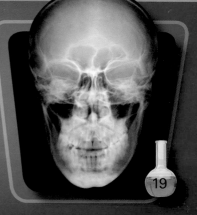

19

"Okay, class," Ms. Solution called the class to order. "Now you understand about groups. For homework, please find out what other elements are in your group. Find out what they have in common."

"Maybe we could work in groups," cracked Kenny.

Ms. Solution laughed with a snort. "Good idea," she said. Then she handed a red-flowered paper-towel roll to Lisa.

"Lisa, take the end of this roll and pass it to Ben. It should unravel all the way along your row until it reaches Neville's neon (Ne)."

When the students finished this, Ms. Solution said, "Everyone holding the red-flowered roll is in the same **period** in the periodic table. This is the 'across' part of the crossword puzzle. As with groups, elements in a period share similar properties. You keen observers will note that Lisa's element is a 3, and the numbers follow in order across to Neville's 10. We'll solve the mystery of those numbers next week!"

Chemists worked long and hard to find the first elements. Then they worked to classify the elements, which means to organize them into groups according to their properties. These early scientists ran many experiments so they could determine how elements might be alike. Because these experiments sometimes caused explosions, chemists had a reputation for being "mad" or insane. They risked life and limb to classify elements!

SHOCKER

The element nitrogen (N) makes up 78 percent of our air. It is essential for life. However, when joined with other elements, nitrogen is also a component of **acid rain** and dynamite!

boron (5)   carbon (6)   nitrogen (7)

ELEMENTary Fact

Eight elements make up more than 98 percent of the earth. Oxygen makes up about half of it. The other main elements, in order of largest to smallest percentage, are: silicon, aluminum, iron, calcium, sodium, potassium, and magnesium.

Amethyst crystals contain silicon, oxygen, and iron.

I find it helps to keep turning back to the diagram on page 11. This way, I can quickly check and confirm my assumptions. I was right – it is like a crossword puzzle!

oxygen (8)

fluorine (9)

neon (10)

TRANSFORMED BY FIRE

On Thursday morning, Ms. Solution brought in some iron filings. She asked Celia to show the class how the iron filings could be picked up with a magnet. After that, she lit a **Bunsen burner**. "Keep back, students," she warned them. Then she sprinkled the iron filings over the flame. There was a hissing, crackling noise, and tiny sparks of light burst from the flame.

"The flame has transformed our iron filings into something called iron oxide," Ms. Solution told the class. Next she asked Kenny to use the magnet to pick up the tiny pieces of burned iron that had fallen from the flame. Kenny tried, but nothing happened. They were not attracted to the magnet.

"Fire changes the properties of whatever it heats," Ms. Solution explained. "It is fire that makes chemistry possible!

"Some of the earliest people to use chemistry weren't scientists like me," she said. "They were prehistoric people learning to use fire. They discovered that fire could turn flour and other ingredients into bread, and that it could turn clay into pottery. They even discovered that it could help them turn metallic rocks, such as iron ore, into powerful weapons."

Fireworks get their spark and colors from the earth's elements. Lithium (Li) adds red, and sodium (Na) adds yellow or gold. Tiny iron (Fe) filings are added to sparklers to make them sparkle.

SHOCKER

Iron (Fe) is a component of both steel and blood! We need iron in our blood to help transport oxygen around the body. If we don't eat enough iron-rich foods, we become ill.

ELEMENTary Fact

The element neon (Ne) is a gas. It is used to make signs glow. A glass tube of neon gas produces a bright red or orange color when an electric current passes through it. If a tiny amount of mercury is added to the neon, the gases glow blue.

GLORIOUS GOLD AND OTHER MARVELOUS METALS

Next, Ms. Solution placed a silver jewelry box on her desk. Out of it, she pulled a gold medallion. She rubbed it near the sunny window so that the students could see glimmers of sparkling gold.

"Gold is a metallic element." Ms. Solution said, twirling her medallion. "It is very soft for a metal. It makes a useless weapon or tool! Yet, because gold is so beautiful and doesn't **tarnish**, more people have fought over this metal than any other. Wars have started over gold. Governments have been toppled. America was explored by people crazed about finding gold!"

Next Ms. Solution stuck seven photos on the whiteboard. "Ancient people knew only seven metals," she said. "They were gold, silver, iron, mercury, tin, copper, and lead. Can you figure out which metal is which in these photos? Here are some clues. Mercury is liquid at everyday temperatures. Silver develops a black tarnish when exposed to air. Copper conducts heat, so it makes excellent cookware. Tin was once used to make toys. Lead is a heavy, gray metal, and iron turns reddish brown when it rusts."

This heading is an example of the use of alliteration – the repetition of the same sounds at the beginning of words. Authors use this device to make their writing more interesting.

Before there were chemists, there were alchemists. Alchemists believed that gold was the perfect substance. They thought that if they could learn to make it, the process would lead them to wisdom. In their search, they mixed many substances together. We now know that gold is an element and so it can't be made out of other elements.

Ancient Babylonian bronze head from about 2250 B.C.

Alchemists in the Middle Ages

About 5,500 years ago, people discovered how to make bronze by melting together copper and arsenic. Later they learned to make it from copper and tin. Bronze is called an alloy. This means that it is a combination of a metal and one or more other elements.

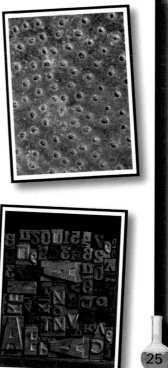

NAME THE METALS!

UP AND ATOM!

Ms. Solution began Friday's class with a question. "Do you know what an **atom** is?" she asked the class.

A few students raised their hands. Ms. Solution called on Allie, who guessed that an atom was something really small. Then Ben said that he thought atoms were used to make other things.

"Well, you're both right," said Ms. Solution. "An atom is the smallest part of an element that can still be identified as that element. For example, we know that gold is an element. A solid-gold medallion is made up of millions of gold atoms.

The center of an atom is called its nucleus. It contains tiny particles called protons, which have a positive electric charge. It also contains tiny particles called neutrons, which have no charge. Around the outside are really, REALLY tiny negative charges called electrons."

Ms. Solution reminded everyone about the numbers on their cards. "Remember how the numbers were in order from Lisa all the way to Neville? Well, the whole table is in numerical order. Each number tells us how many protons are in the nucleus of that element. Hydrogen, for example, has one proton. Helium has two protons, and gold has 79 protons.

An atom usually has an equal number of protons and electrons. The number of neutrons, however, can vary. Look at the square for gold (Au) on the periodic table."

SHOCKER

An atom is more than a million times smaller than a grain of salt, but it is held together with a large amount of energy. Atomic bombs are made by breaking the nuclei of many uranium (U) or plutonium (Pu) atoms to release their energy.

Parts of an Atom
- nucleus   center of the atom
- proton   particle with a positive charge
- neutron   particle with no charge
- electron   particle with a negative charge

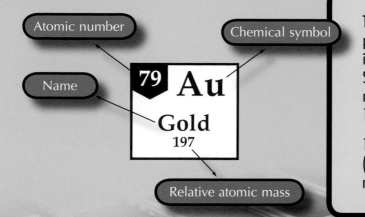

Atomic number

Chemical symbol

Name

79 Au

Gold

197

Relative atomic mass

The atomic mass is the number of protons plus the number of neutrons in an atom. Mass is similar to weight. Since gold has 79 protons, we can use math to figure out that it usually has 118 neutrons.

197 – 79 = 118
(atomic mass – number of protons = number of neutrons)

This diagram shows how scientists sometimes draw atoms. In the center is the nucleus. It is made up of protons (red) and neutrons (green). Tiny electrons (blue) whizz around the outside of the nucleus. The electrons have a negative charge, which attracts them to the protons' positive charge.

JOINING UP

On Monday, Ms. Solution smiled as she walked among the desks.

"I'd like Sodium and Chlorine to stand together at the front," she said. Nathan and Cleo did as instructed.

"Any ideas what we have here?" asked Ms. Solution.

"Boyfriend and girlfriend?" suggested Kenny. Cleo blushed, and Nathan looked annoyed.

"Any *sensible* ideas?" asked Ms. Solution. But no one could think of anything to suggest.

"What we have here is salt!" said Ms. Solution. "That's right. When a sodium atom and a chlorine atom join together, they become a **compound** called sodium chloride. Scientists write it as NaCl. But most of us just call it salt."

One atom of sodium joined to one atom of chlorine makes one **molecule** of sodium chloride.

11
Na
Sodium

17
Cl
Chlorine

Next, Ms. Solution walked across the room and turned on a faucet.

"Here's another compound," she said. "Who knows what it is?"

"Water!" said Kenny.

"Yes," said Ms. Solution. "But what elements is it made up of?"

Celia took a guess. "Is it H and O? I've heard people call water H_2O."

"Good job, Celia," said Ms. Solution. "Scientists call water H_2O because it's a compound of hydrogen (H) and oxygen (O). The numeral 2 after the H means that there are two atoms of hydrogen joined to every one atom of oxygen. When elements join together to become compounds, their properties change. Hydrogen and oxygen are gases, but when they join to become water, they change into a liquid."

This cube-shaped crystal is a grain of salt (NaCl) seen under a microscope.

ELEMENTary Fact

Different compounds can be made from the same elements. For example, H_2O is water, but H_2O_2 is hydrogen peroxide, a chemical that lightens hair. CO_2 is carbon dioxide, the gas we breathe out, but CO is carbon monoxide, a poisonous gas.

Scientists now make previously undiscovered, high-atomic-number elements artificially in labs. Scientists use a machine called a particle accelerator to make two light elements crash into each other. The hope is that when the elements crash, the protons will join to form a new, heavier element. Most of the recently created elements have fallen to pieces within a second of forming.

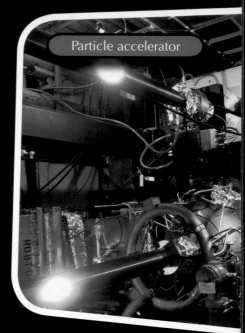

Particle accelerator

WHAT DO YOU THINK?

Many dollars are spent in the quest to find new elements. Is the pursuit of new elements worthwhile, or should we spend money on other types of science?

PRO

I think we need to learn whatever we can about our world and the universe. Maybe an element will be created that can help the earth. For example, it might help us generate energy in a safe, renewable way. We just don't know unless scientists study this.

Let's look at this mathematically. To make element 118, scientists shot calcium into californium. In the experiment, calcium's 20 protons joined with californium's 98 protons, creating an atom with 118 protons. However, element 118 survived only for part of a second before falling apart. Some scientists say that, someday, elements might be made or discovered that are heavier, live longer lives, and have exciting new properties. In 1941, scientists created an element that proved to have a use. It was a form of plutonium. Plutonium has been used as fuel for atomic bombs. It's also been used in nuclear reactors at power plants.

CON

I think we should be focusing on other things, such as medicine and the environment. I would rather spend our money on these things than on finding new elements that might be used to make something wasteful or destructive.

GLOSSARY

acid rain rain containing acids that have come from polluted air

alkaline the opposite of acidic; able to react with an acid to form water and a salt.

bacteria (*bak TEER ee yah*) tiny living things too small to be seen without a microscope

Bunsen burner a small gas burner commonly used in laboratories

chemical reaction a process that changes one or more substances into one or more different substances

compound a substance made up of atoms of two or more elements linked together

conduct to allow electricity to flow

density the weight of an object in relation to its size; a measure of how closely packed the molecules are

dissolve to mix completely with a liquid

malleable (*MAL ee uh buhl*) easy to shape

mass the amount of matter of which something is made up

matter a substance; any solid, liquid, or gas

metal a hard, shiny, malleable substance, such as iron, copper, or gold. Metals conduct heat and electricity.

metallic made of metal

nonmetal any substance that is not a metal

period a row of elements in the periodic table of elements

semimetal a substance that has some of the properties of a metal to a small degree but is not malleable

solution a liquid with another substance dissolved in it

tarnish the dulling of the surface of a metal caused by a chemical reaction with a substance such as oxygen

Metal

FIND OUT MORE

BOOKS

Meiani, Antonella. *Chemistry*. Lerner Publications Company, 2002.

Miller, Ron. *The Elements*. Twenty-First Century Books, 2005.

Newmark, Anne and Buller, Laura. *Chemistry*. DK Children, 2005.

Richardson, Hazel. *How to Split the Atom*. Franklin Watts, 2001.

Wiker, Benjamin. *The Mystery of the Periodic Table*. Bethlehem Books, 2003.

Zannos, Susan. *Dmitri Mendeleyev and the Periodic Table*. Mitchell Lane Publishers, 2004.

WEB SITES

Go to the Web sites below to learn more about the periodic table of elements.

www.chem4kids.com

www.chemicalelements.com

www.mcwdn.org/chemist/chemist.html

http://library.thinkquest.org/J001539

INDEX

ABOUT THE AUTHOR

Laura Layton Strom is the author of many nonfiction and fiction books for children. When she is not writing books, she helps publishers and other authors create educational books.
Laura got her first microscope when she was eight years old, and she still loves learning and reading about science. She wishes that Ms. Solution had been her chemistry teacher.

DATE DUE